Mind Candy

WAYNE NICHOLAS HOFFMAN

Published by:

Hoffman Entertainment Inc.

info@ilovehoffman.com

Design by: Wayne Nicholas Hoffman

Hoffman Entertainment® website: www.ilovehoffman.com

ISBN-13: 978-1477487631

ISBN-10: 1477487638

First Edition, May 2012

For Wayne Shifflett

Without you, the man who wrote this book would not exist.

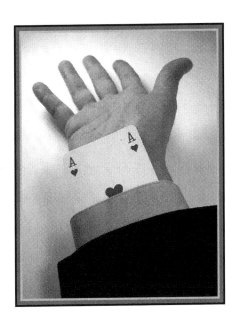

CONTENTS

ACKNOWLEDGMENTS

I'd like to acknowledge you.
Yes, you.

1. INTRODUCTION

This is the first sentence of a book that has been in the making for 29 years. As I'm writing this I'm sitting in an airport in San Jose, Costa Rica waiting to board a flight with a final destination of Los Angeles, California. There was no real reason for me to start typing at this exact moment. It wasn't planned. It was just time to put this story and knowledge in the hands of others. The only way I can describe the feeling I have right now is to compare it to scratching an itch, one that you've had for a really long time. If you're reading this then you are one of the few people that I had in mind when I sat down and began typing. I hope the words you're about to read will evoke some type of emotional, physical, and/or spiritual reaction from you that will in the end make you learn something about the world around you and more importantly, about yourself.

The start of this book was inspired by an email I recently received from a good friend. It read as follows:

"Hi Wayne,

The more I see, the more I'm impressed. I know a lot of people, and most would say I've had more of an adventure with my life than they have. But you -- dude, sweet Jesus!

You need to write a book describing in intimate detail what it is that sets you apart from the average person, and why it is that you are living a life most people would describe as a fantasy. If I didn't know you personally, I'd hardly believe it.

We've talked about this stuff a lot, but some of the shit that comes out of your mouth still leaves me skeptical. I'll never forget when you said you thought my buddy from Ghana (where I suppose you've been now, even if you were only passing through) could be an astronaut if he wanted to. I mean, give me a break.

I can't get my head around that, but whatever you're doing and believing is obviously working for you.

Good fortune plays a role -- you're young, healthy, handsome, smart, and capable -- but a lot of people are those things, including me. That could not possibly account for more than 2% of it.

Knowing exactly what you wanted very early in life and getting an early start certainly helped as well, but that still doesn't explain why you DID get an early start and so many others (most, in fact) didn't

I hope you're taking notes dude, because you have a book here. I'm serious. Find the time and write it. Make sure you address those who are not satisfied with easy optimism (like me) and you'll have a good one. Anticipate the obvious objections, deal with them in a satisfactory way, and you could teach a lot of people a lot of things.

The last thing the world needs is another self-help book, but f@$k it. Yours would be good. You surely have a lot of stories and anecdotes from the road by now, so use those to give the book a narrative structure. Along the way, make your case.

And if you need an editor, look me up. I'm just getting a start, so I wouldn't charge much.

        Nick"

A lot of people have asked me what the secret is to leading a life like mine. I always take it as a compliment and feel like it's necessary to give all of those people the real answer. It just so happens that you are now along for the ride. For the past two decades (probably longer by the time you're reading this) I've been traveling around this crazy planet we call Earth. On my journey I've had the fortune of leading a life that defies logic and seems to boarder on fictional. On top of that I've had the luxury of earning money from doing things I enjoy.

To give you a taste of what I'm referring to, let me give you a flashflood of information to stimulate your palate before we move on. Let me preface this by saying what you are about to read is not an attempt to boast or serve my ego. It's merely giving you information that might expose the reason why people have asked me for my secret. You may find some the things I'm about to share impressive, while I'm sure some of you may not find any value in the things I'm about to share. Either way, these are the things that were the catalyst for my writing this book. So, I share the following with great fervor.

At the moment my world consists of jet setting around the globe to various tropical and exotic locales at other's expense. When I'm not traveling I spend time at my amazing home in Los Angeles and call major celebrities neighbors and friends. I own an extremely successful entertainment company that boasts major profits. I have close personal relationships with some of the greatest friends a man could have while maintaining loving relationships with my family. I have found a sense of inner peace and a calm that surrounds my life. I can go where I want to go, when I want to go there, and I answer to nobody except for myself. (I'll leave the idea of God out of this as to not bring religion into my story. I heard religion and politics are bad conversation topics.)

I've performed on television and radio stations around the world and continue to do so. I've been in more limousines than I can count and have paid for very few of them. I have an art collection that includes some of the world's masters. If I sold them it would pay for my high-end sports car a million times over. I have had the pleasure of becoming a motivational speaker; I've worked as a life coach for people, and as a result have positively affected their lives. The material things I own and the non-material things that

I foster continue to grow and evolve into a living dream. I think you get the point. Now, what does this mean for you? It means you can have anything you want and I'm going to show you how to obtain it. Read that last sentence again slowly.

Before we dive right into the good stuff let's have a little foreplay. This will give you a realistic view of my life. I want you to understand that I am a human being just like you and I have had the same struggles that most people have had. There is nothing special about me. I wasn't born rich, I'm not attractive in my opinion, and I never won the lottery. I'm just a regular guy with a sub-par upbringing.

I started my life with humble beginnings, as most adventurous stories go. I was born to a mother who scraped through life earning money as a waitress and my father was a blue-collar worker who spent most of his life in an aluminum foundry. I surely wasn't born with a silver spoon in my mouth. It had more of an aluminum flavor to it. With that said, I didn't have much advantage over any of my peers growing up. In fact, as I look back, I was probably at somewhat of a disadvantage compared to most. I can still remember going to thrift stores to buy my clothes while I watched most of the other kids sport the newest fashions. Being an extremely skinny kid didn't help either. The teasing words still sear through my mind even today. Welcome to being an adolescent.

My parents were divorced before I was conscious of the world. I never saw them together as a couple. In my world, parents didn't live together, let alone like each other. I can't say it's a rare thing anymore as the divorce rate is speeding past a fifty percent rate at the moment. My mother took on the roll of raising me and my father had the cliché visitation ordered by the court. However, I can say that both of them have had a profound effect on my ideals, my mentality, and the words you're reading.

My father was the consummate pessimist. Maybe I should more affectionately call him a "realist." His view of the world always consisted of what might go wrong and/or why I shouldn't do something remotely adventurous. Ever cautious, my father lived a life that most would consider to be a wonderful definition of the word "safe". I always wonder if that was from the tough upbringing he had or if it was a mentality he formed on his own. An abusive father who was an alcoholic raised him and that man was the grandfather I never knew. Considering my father had me at what most would consider being an old age, my grandparents on his side of my family passed away before I was even born. My father, although a pessimist, (sorry, "realist") had a vivacious attitude and was always the one to get people laughing. He is definitely an outgoing person. My dad would always speak his mind and never cared about what people thought. This sometimes led to embarrassing situations for me, while at the same time provided hundreds of stories. I could write a whole book of them. Maybe I'll start that one at another airport.

My mother led a conventional life with hints of optimism and a passion for the arts. She had a rough upbringing herself, however it didn't seem to affect her in a way that negatively affected her adult life. Her outlet was dance. For many years my mother was a professional ballroom dancer and went on to win awards at various competitions. She was a sweet soul who in her later years would become one of the most loving individuals to walk the earth. I'm fighting back tears as I write this. She was always the optimist and had encouraging words whenever you needed them.

Both of them had a differing view of the world that instilled in me what I would consider to be a wonderful combination of levelheadedness and hopefulness. I think that fact also had a lot to do with their divorce. With this view of the world I charged forward not knowing where my life would take me. Looking at where I am now, I would imagine the wide-eyed boy I once was, would never truly be able to imagine the adventure that would come to be his destiny.

Now for the point of this self-described background check: You can come from any beginnings, poor, lower class, middle-class, or extremely wealthy. Regardless of where you come from you can achieve great success in both your personal life and your business life. To give you an analogy let's take a look at the popular casino game of roulette. If you're not familiar with the game, let me give you a quick overview. In roulette you are given a choice to place your bet on any number from one through thirty-six. You can also choose to place your bet on zero or in some cases double zero, but let's not bother with details. The casino dealer then spins a wheel with those numbers printed on it. The dealer will then drop a small ball onto the wheel.

Eventually, as the wheel slows, the ball will land on one of the numbers. If you bet on that number you win. That's the simplified version.

In roulette the casino will display a running list of the numbers that have recently come up. Many people will look at that list of numbers and use it to calculate on which number they will bet on next. For example, a player might see that the number "twenty" hasn't come up in a long time and therefore bet on that number in hopes that it will come up. Most of the time people will assume that a number that hasn't come up recently is "due" to come up soon. They are wasting their time.

The fact of the matter is regardless of what numbers have come up in the past, they have no influence on any of the future numbers selected. The odds never change, just as your odds of success have nothing to do with your past. You cannot use your upbringing as an excuse for your failure to succeed. In the same way you can't use being born rich and good looking as an indicator that you will be successful. I know right now many of the realists reading this are writhing in their seats. Stop for a moment and let your mind ponder this thought: The past doesn't exist anymore. The only thing that truly affects your life from this point forward are the thoughts and actions that you are currently engaged in and the thoughts and actions you will potentially engage in.

This is where the difference between successful individuals and unsuccessful individuals is created. It is in this current moment of cognition that you are deciding your fate. If you are open to the possibility of understanding and opening your mind to this concept then you have at least enough to help create unyielding happiness and success. Stop for a moment and truly contemplate the idea that you can have any type of future you want based upon this precise moment. Look at the time right now. It is only in this moment and in the future moments of your life that you can manipulate and control, unless, of course, you have the ability to time travel. In which case, just please travel back to May 12th, 2011 and go to the San Jose airport in Costa Rica, gate five. Be there at 4:43pm sharp. You'll see me in a black sport coat and a black and grey hat. We'll have this discussion in person.

Just as in roulette your mind wants you to believe that your upbringing, current social status, financial situation, and likewise have a significant effect on your future. Please notice I said "significant." As my father may have pointed out, your past has an effect on your memory or your current state. There's no doubt about it. My secret however, is to realize that those memories and past events are never as significant and effective as the dreams and future events that you will currently create. When you understand this concept you have a weapon that can forge any vision you can create.

"Whether you think you can or can't, you're right"

-Henry Ford."

2. Amnesia

Imagine right now I walk up to you and hit you over the head with a lead pipe. Imagine the splitting pain you would feel moments before you hit the ground and passed out, unconscious. Now imagine waking up. In fact try this exercise: Close your eyes when you read the word "GO" printed below and keep them closed for about at least 5 to 10 seconds. When you open them try to truly imagine that you wake up with amnesia. You have no idea where you are or what your name is. You don't know what book is in front of you. You have no recollection of your past at all. Everything you see around you is brand new and you are seeing it for the first time. Go ahead try it. When you're finished processing the emotions of that feeling come back to reality and continue reading. It's a wild experience. 3........2.........1.......GO.

Good morning. You have no idea where you are. You have no idea what you're reading right now or why. If you'd like to know your name you can check your wallet for an ID. Let me explain. You just woke up from a self-induced amnesia that is going to change your life for the better. You are about to create the life of your dreams. From this point forward you can achieve anything that you want. Nothing is stopping you. My name is Wayne Hoffman and I'm the author of the book you're reading right now. Everything you're about to read was created for you so that you can clear your mind and focus on obtaining the life you deserve. The life YOU create.

You have nothing but your future in that mindset. Nothing from your past matters at all. It has no effect on your future. Everything you do now and from this moment forward are the only things that will truly affect your life. Go through life with self-prescribed amnesia. You own the world. Nobody can stop you.

3. Choose Positive

In this moment you are creating thoughts and emotions that will lead to actions. Those actions will determine your future. If you begin to create negative thoughts, those thoughts will create negative actions and negative conversations that will surround and consume you. The opposite is also true. If you lead a life that focuses on maintaining a positive attitude then you will surely have positive conversations with people and perform positive actions. Imagine a man who wants to be a rock star. He has the option of believing he's not talented enough and that there is no way he'll ever amount to anything. He will probably use those thoughts to create excuses for not trying. He will also tell other people that he believes he's not good enough. In thinking that he is directly communicating those ideas and emotions to those that surround him. After that, those people will then, consciously and subconsciously, begin to agree with him and won't think about the matter any further. The other option for our hypothetical character is to believe he can be successful and that he is extremely talented. He will then communicate that idea to his family, friends, and business partners. Those people will begin to believe he may be talented and might have a chance to succeed.

Think about your past. Surely there has been a moment in your life where a friend of yours has asked you if you could recommend a good product or service. Maybe they asked you to recommend a nice restaurant or a talented disc jockey for a wedding. You probably gave them a suggestion based upon your emotional connection and experience with that restaurant or DJ. Now let's use our hypothetical rock star and add him to this situation. If someone asks you if you could recommend someone who is in the music industry you will have one of two thoughts based around our rock star's mentality. You will either think, "I know a guy who is really dedicated and driven" or you will think "I can't recommend the guy because he doesn't even believe in himself." It is for this reason that the mentality that you carry with you on a daily basis is pinnacle to your success. If you carry a positive attitude with you and believe you will have wild success, then you will inevitably communicate that to others. It is the people who surround you that facilitate your success.

Take a moment to ponder this idea: If there were no other human beings on this planet, could you achieve the things you have achieved? The answer is no. Those that surround us facilitate most of the tangible successes we have. The importance of your thoughts and how they affect the thoughts and actions of the people around you are paramount to your future. Start believing you can accomplish anything and you will move toward that. It is the interactions with the people that surround you that can help make your dreams come true.

4. The Four Steps

Now that we have established that principle, let's take a look at an effective method to take the fast track to success. Over the years I have developed a system that takes positive thoughts and turns them into instant physical realities. It is this system that has given me a life that, in my opinion, has been extremely rewarding. The system is based upon more than just "the power of positive thinking" and applies tried-and-true business tactics to make your thoughts turn into realities. I implement the use of business tactics in my system to help structure your positive thoughts and feelings. The system that I call the "Hoffman System" is a four-step process that enables you to make your dreams come true. Here are the four basic steps:

1. Feel

2. Define

3. Plan

4. Do

An easy way to remember the four steps is to use the acronym F.D.P.D. I like to think "Fire Department, Police Department." Learning and living these four steps on a daily basis will produce amazing results in your personal and professional life. Feel free to think of ways to use this system in every area of your life to improve its quality.

The First Step: FEEL

The first step is to feel. Everything we gain in life is derived from a feeling. We eat because we feel hungry, we cry because we're sad, we sleep because we feel tired, we scream because we're angry, and we have sex because we feel aroused. The last time you decided to take a nap is because you felt tired. These feelings can be emotional feelings or physical feelings. Often times these will overlap. The last time you were emotionally depressed it almost certainly caused you to feel physically disabled. It's these feelings that drive us toward the things we achieve, whether that is a large bank account or a tasty piece of cake.

Many people have the problem of liking the idea of having something versus truly wanting and more importantly needing something. For example, many people often say, "It would great to be rich. I could buy whatever I want" or "It would be so cool to be famous." Those are thoughts, not feelings. Thoughts like those are often sparked by outside influences, such as, seeing a nice sports car at a car dealership or watching a show about celebrities. Feelings that are generated from the inside are the ones that will determine your future. You have to truly desire something in order to achieve. If you make a list of things that would be nice to have and a list of things that you will absolutely achieve, the list of things that would be nice to have has a smaller chance of becoming reality when compared to the other list. So to recap, you must first truly desire your vision to realistically move toward it. You must feel it.

Imagine the face of someone you love. Picture them standing in front of you. This person might be a spouse, a parent, or possibly a child. Imagine the clothes they would be wearing. Imagine their smile. Hear their laugh in your mind. Truly imagine them standing in front of you. Now imagine a stranger walks up and punches them in the face. How do you feel? How would you react? What would you do? I imagine that your reaction would be similar to mine. You would beat the shit out of them. You feel upset. You would feel angry. That same inner dialogue is what will carry you toward living your dreams. Without that inner strength you can't overcome the hurdles that will come to discourage you. The feeling will inevitably get you past the speed bumps that will block your path.

Success is not just moving toward a goal. One of the most important, and unrecognized, areas of reaching goals is the ability to overcome obstacles. I truly believe this is where most people fail in their attempts to succeed. In fact, the difference between those of you that will succeed and those that will fail will be the ability to feel such emotion that you cannot be deterred. The ones reading this sentence who really recognize the fact that many obstacles will come your way are the ones who will be successful. There will be problems. I repeat, there will be problems. The most damaging problems are the mental blocks that come from yourself. You are truly the only one who can stop you from reaching your full potential. The sad thing is that most people don't realize it. They like to feel defeated and blame it on others during times of stress and negativity.

You can overcome anything if you recognize that you have the power to choose how you feel about problems that come your way. You need to have an internal reminder that you are in control of your destiny. You are the one who feels the positive energy flowing through your body and mind. The rest of the world is your playground. When you have true intent and you recognize it's power, then you will not only have the ability to succeed, but you will have the unstoppable force at your fingertips that will guarantee that you succeed.

$$1+1+1+1+1+1+1+1+1+1+1+1+1+1+1+1+1 \times 0 = ?$$

A lot of action multiplied by no feeling equals nothing.

The Second Step: DEFINE

The second step is Define. You have to define what you want before you can have it. Many people say that they want to be "successful." The problem is that they don't define what their version of success really is. Does being successful mean having a huge mansion? Does it mean having seven sports cars? Does it mean having close relationships with your family? What exactly is success to you? Using that analogy as a guide, think about what you want in life and ask yourself if you have truly defined it. Most people think they have defined it but really have not. Many people say their goal is to be rich. But what is rich? You have to think about what exact amount of money must you see on your bank statement to consider yourself rich. Is it $200,000? $1,000,000,000? You must define the exact situation you want to experience in your life in order to turn it into a reality. You have to have a goal to hit it.

If you're like me, a mental picture might help you better understand this concept. Imagine a soccer game. However in this scenario imagine a soccer field without any nets; In other words, no goals. What would you see during the game? You would see a bunch of guys running around kicking a ball back and forth. It would look like they're playing a game, but they wouldn't be getting anywhere. The same holds true for life. If you don't define your goals you will go through life kicking around the ball, feeling like your advancing, but in reality you will be going nowhere. Take the time to extraordinarily break down your goals and define what they truly are.

One of the hurdles you may face is defining a goal that you think you want, but actually don't want. You want the result of your goal. One of the things I talk to my clients about is why they want to have certain things in their life. One of my clients told me they wanted to be famous. When I asked them why she answered, "So I can have tons of money." When I asked her why she wanted tons of money she responded, "So I can travel the world." What she failed to realize is that her true goal wasn't to be famous. Her true end goal was to travel. After that moment of reflection we sat down and analyzed whether or not she could find a sense of accomplishment by traveling without the hassle of the paparazzi chasing after her. The look on her face when she had that epiphany was priceless. "You're right" she said. "I don't want to be famous at all, in fact, the idea of being famous is horrible! I just want to travel!"

With all of these things in mind, make sure you sit down in a quiet place and write down what your goals are. After you write them down take a moment to break them down and specify the details of each goal. After that, write down why you want to achieve each goal and what type of satisfaction you'll receive from achieving each. This simple exercise will help bring clarity to your life and help move you through the Hoffman System.

I want you to imagine you and I are about to go to dinner. Picture us sitting at a table in your favorite restaurant. Now picture yourself looking at the menu. Now picture yourself never ordering any food. What will happen? No food will come. This is where most people live life, looking at the menu. The problem appears when people see the menu their whole life but don't order. This is why defining what you want becomes so important. If you continuously look at all the things our world has to offer but don't put your precise order into the universe, then you will never receive the awesome things that you desire.

When you eat at a restaurant you give extra attention to your order with phrases such as, "I'd like it medium rare please" or "Can you put the sauce on the side?" Don't you think you should put as much if not more energy in defining how you want your life? Take the time to define what it is you want and how you want it. It is in these moments of definition that your future is forged.

Another good analogy is to compare it to a sculptor who has a block of stone in front of him. Most often the sculptor will know what they want to sculpt before they pick up the hammer and chisel. They will have a vision of what they want to create from the beginning. They define their vision and then begin to sculpt the formless stone into their vision. Step by step they release the potential of the stone to reveal a magnificent creation. In the same way, you should release your own vision of the future by first defining it. Get specific. After you get specific, get even more specific. Boil it down until you can't get any more detail out of your vision. It is then that you hold the power to create your perfect life.

An Interlude Exercise

Imagine your life is a movie. Imagine you turn on the TV and are in the middle of the movie. Picture a scene in the movie where you're reading a motivating book. Look around right now. The location you are in right now is the set of the movie. Imagine the first part of the script contained all of the things that have happened in your past. That script has led you to this moment right here, right now. How would it play out from this point forward? What would happen in your life from this point forward if you were the author of the script? Now stop. Take a moment to realize you *are* the author. You are the one who gets to choose how your life manifests from this moment forward.

The clearer you can imagine your movie, the more likely your vision will become a reality. It's exercise that will intensify and define your goals. You may have briefly attempted this exercise as you read it. However, sit down when you have a good amount of time and try this. Don't do it when you're about to rush off somewhere nor while you're lying down and about to fall asleep, because you'll do just that. Do it when you have a substantial amount of time and a clear mind. After you're finished take a moment to write down the things that stood out in your mind. Keep a detailed note of each of the wonderful things you imagined coming into your life. Were you married? Single? Living in the mountains or the city? Who were your friends? How did you feel? What made you feel that way?

Practicing this exercise several times throughout the year will help you redefine your vision. Keep in mind that as we grow our goals and dreams change. I'm sure you can think back to a time when you were a child and had dreams of becoming a doctor or a veterinarian. Have your goals changed since then? If you're like most people then your vision of the future has changed many times. Keeping this in mind, make sure you "play your movie" often.

The Importance of Defining

The importance of defining your goals is significant not only for clarification but to ensure ultimate success. An often-unrecognized problem is the human tendency to take the path of least resistance. This is a theory you probably remember from school. Electricity has the same tendency. In reality, it's more than just a tendency; it's a fact of science. Humans like to do the same thing. Sometimes, however, this leads us to become comfortable when we reach a marginal level of success. If I were to hand you $1,000,000 in cash right now you would probably be ecstatic. You would probably call all of your family members, perhaps quit your job, and relax in comfort. But the problem arises when you consider that obtaining $1,000,000 was not your goal. Maybe you wanted to do more. Granted, having that money would make you comfortable, but it wouldn't make you fulfill your goals and reach your higher purpose.

I'm writing this from personal experience. I once, not too long ago, reached a point of comfort in my career. I was touring the world with my show, I had stable income, I was interacting with my family and friends, and things were good. But that was the problem. Things were good, but they weren't where I truly wanted them to be. The vision of what I wanted my life to be was far greater than what it was. The problem was, from the outside, not a problem at all. In fact, even from the inside I felt a great sense of comfort, but there was part of me that knew that I hadn't attained the greatness that I was destined for. An analogy I can describe that matches this moment would be an attempt to climb to the summit of Mount Everest.

I could prepare for months, go through training, and climb 80% to the top. When I get home I could tell all my friends that I climbed Mount Everest. The truth is that I didn't reach the summit, but I climbed Mount Everest. Deep within myself I would know that I didn't obtain my ultimate goal. Although I could be comfortable in telling my friends I participated in a great feat, there would be a deep feeling of failure. Keep true to your ultimate goals and don't settle for less.

The point of this visualization is to remind you to keep your goals in mind even when you hit major milestones that get you closer to your ultimate goal. Don't get comfortable with being just "good". Make a pact with yourself to go beyond the level of "comfortably good" and reach your ultimate level of greatness. Become the ultimate YOU.

The Third Step: PLAN

After you define your goals you have to plan a method to achieve them. A great way to break down your goals into actions is to use an idea that I learned from famed speaker and author David Allen. Ask yourself "What is the next doable action I can take?" If you think about the things on your to-do list you will see that most of the things you write down aren't actually things you can physically do. For example, if your car breaks down you might put "Fix Car" on your to-do list. However, unless you're going out to your car to fix it yourself, you can't actually do that. So let's reevaluate it. You have to make an appointment at a garage, but you don't have their phone number. However, your friend Wayne recommended a great garage to you. Therefore, the next doable action is to pick up the phone and call Wayne to get the number for the garage. Writing "Fix Car" is a lot different than writing "Call Wayne", however, you get a much clearer understanding of what must actually be done in order to achieve your goal.

Using the question of "What is the next doable action?" is a wonderful way of defining your goals. This mentality is a key factor in the system and you will find great power in asking such a simple question. In fact, right now I want you to think about something on your to-do list. This might be as simple as picking up groceries or as complex as the project you're involved in at work. Got something? Now ask yourself what the next action is that you can take to get closer to labeling that project "complete". If you actually thought about it then you are probably feeling a sense of relief right now. You have just gotten a little closer to your goal just by asking that one question.

One of things to remember is that not all actions are physical. Keep in mind that your goals might involve one of the two other important areas of life. Thinking and waiting. If you have to create something to complete your goal, then you will have to take time to think. A good friend of mine, Jeff Yalden, wears a bracelet that has the phrase "Take Time To Think" embossed across it. Taking time to think about things is an often forgotten part of a healthy and successful life. Taking time to think and create is something that needs to be scheduled. I highly recommend scheduling time to think about the projects that are in your life. These projects can be personal or business oriented. Taking time to think about your family and their needs, taking time to think about yourself and your own needs, and taking the time to think about business are all important parts of moving toward becoming the ultimate you.

The other action people tend to ignore is the power of waiting. You may see the next thing on your to-do list is to call someone so you can get information from him or her. When you physically call the person you may have to leave them a message. Likewise, if you email them you may have to wait for a response. Therefore, your next doable action is "Wait for so-and-so to respond". One problem I used to encounter is the reality that sometimes people don't respond in a timely manner or at all. Rather than waiting forever, make sure you ponder what action you must take if they don't respond quickly or at all. What will you do? How can you move the project ahead? Finding that answer while you wait is a massively important tool that you will no doubt use on a regular basis. Have patience…but not too much.

An Interlude Story

A few years ago I was sitting in my corporate office with my manager discussing my future plans for performing. We were discussing my upcoming tour and the idea of international markets. He asked me where I wanted to go next. I blurted out "Trinidad and Tobago." At the time I had no reason to say it. For some reason it was in the back of my mind to go there. I didn't know why. It was just a feeling.

A few months later I was in Trinidad and Tobago checking into my room. Lying on the counter was a penny. It was local currency. It was at that moment that I realized how I ended up there. The look on my face as I stood at that counter must have been priceless. A flood of emotion ran over me like a monster wave crushing a small boat. Let's rewind about twenty years so you can understand why.

My mother primarily raised me while I was growing up. We found ourselves moving from place to place more often that I'd like to admit. During one short-lived stay at her friend's house I was given an entire room to put my toys. I was also given a large wooden chest in which I could place some of them. At the time I was probably about the age of four or five. I can remember looking deep inside the bottom of the chest and seeing a very small piece of shiny metal wedged between the wood pieces that made the chest. I somehow managed to pry the piece of metal from the crevice to find myself holding a shiny coin.

To a five year old any coin would be exciting to find. This one however was special. It wasn't like the coins I was used to seeing. It was different. I ended up keeping that coin for a very long time. In fact, I believe if I went to my closet filled with objects I hold dear, I would find that coin. It was a special penny that came from a place I had never heard of before. It was from Trinidad and Tobago. On one side of the coin there was a hummingbird emblazoned across it. At that young age I thought I found a coin that had to be worth millions of dollars. The truth was that it was probably worth less than a penny.

For years I kept that coin and its amazing value in the back of my mind. It was the first time I had ever found real treasure, in a treasure chest no less. It was during that discovery that the mythical place of Trinidad and Tobago took hold of a small but powerful part of my brain. I wanted to go to this place and see all of its wonders. Over the next twenty years my memory of the coin faded away and my attention went to the normal adolescent endeavors such as girls, sports, video games, and so on. However, any time someone would mention Trinidad and Tobago my mind would instantly leap back to the coin I had found and the exciting emotion I had when I found it.

I recently realized that because I had such emotion attached to that place, every little action that I was taking was subconsciously leading me there. I realized that any opportunity to travel, would inevitably lead me there. Not because I had a real reason to go there, but because I had such a strong emotional connection with it. It was all of the small actions that led me there. Because the place was in the back of mind and not the forefront, it took me twenty years to get there. Had it been my number one priority in life, I would have been there in a flash.

My life was just like the hummingbird that was pressed onto the back of the coin. As you may know, hummingbirds are amazing birds that fly with unbelievable precision. They flap their wings millions of times per minute in order to hover magically over the flowers that are their food source. It takes them millions of small actions to allow them to progress with their goals. Just like the hummingbird, it took me millions of little actions to get to Trinidad and Tobago and fulfill the young boys desire to visit a magical place. Be like the hummingbird and execute lots of small actions to move toward the bigger picture. Be a hummingbird.

The Fourth Step: DO

If you've felt passionate about a goal, defined exactly what it is, and planned a series of doable actions, the next step is to execute those plans. Most people have an easy time feeling their goals. Defining and planning their goals is most often the difficult part. The last step can either be difficult or effortless depending on your nature. If you tend to worry or procrastinate you might be one of the people this last step is directed toward. I find that many of the people I deal with are afraid of their own success. For example, I dealt with an entertainer who had a goal to appear on a major talk show in the United States. They felt passionate about it, defined what they wanted to see happen, planned the steps to get there, and then froze. They had the phone number of the talent booker for the show but couldn't seem to pick up the phone. They sat with the number saved in their email box for weeks before they encountered their catalyst, yours truly.

When I asked the entertainer why they hadn't called they simply responded "What if they don't want me on the show?" It was a sense of fear that stopped them from getting closer to their goal. It was in that moment that I questioned whether or not they thought it would be nice to be a guest on the show versus having no other option than to be a guest on the show. I notice that people tend to worry about hearing the word "no." One of my colleagues Steve Chandler gave me a wonderful piece of advice that cleared the way for me and helped eliminate fear from my life. He pointed out that "yes" lives in a world of "no." In other words, in order to have people respond with a yes, you will undoubtedly have to receive a no on occasion.

Hearing the word "no" is just a piece of information. Most people attached a story to the word that quite simply isn't true. If you went to a prom during high school you might remember the emotional turmoil revolving around who was going with whom. In my case, the guys traditionally asked the girls to the prom. (I'm excluding our LGBT friends for the sake of ease in writing and clarity) Many of my male friends were extremely nervous to ask a girl to the prom. They figured if they heard "no" that it would mean "No, you're not attractive enough for me to go with you" or perhaps, "No, you aren't intelligent enough and you don't have enough money for me to consider you to be a suitable mate." The fact of the matter is, those statements weren't true. They were fictional stories attached to the potential response.

"Worrying is like paying on a debt that may never come due."

-Will Rogers

One of the analogies Steve used is as follows: Imagine I give you a coin with the challenge that every time you flip the coin and it lands on heads, I will give you $100. Every time it lands on heads you don't win nor lose anything. What would you do? You would flip the hell out of that coin! You wouldn't stop between each flip and say, "I'm worried that it will land on tales and I won't get anything." That would be absurd, right? However, you've been guilty of using that same mentality repeatedly in your life. You didn't ask because you were afraid of hearing "no".

If you want to be successful you have to learn to love the word "no." If you are hearing the word "no" then you are also hearing the word "yes." Yes lives in a world of no. Yes and no are like heads and tales on a coin. You can't have one without the other. Just like you can't have happiness without sadness. If you didn't have sadness you wouldn't have anything to compare happiness to. Learn to love the balance of nature and to not attach false stories to hearing a negative response. A negative response doesn't have to have an emotion attached to it. A negative response is just information. Yes and no are words that we use to communicate an idea.

Take that concept and apply it to your own life. Why do we procrastinate? We do it because we fear the unknown. I personally think much of it stems from our childhood. I can remember a time when I was afraid of the dark. It wasn't a fear of anything in particular. It was a fear of the unknown. I've since beaten my fear of the dark and have the ability to not only be fearless in it, but also enjoy it. Don't fear the unknown and do the actions that will lead to your destiny.

5. An Interesting Anecdote

As I was typing the last page of this book a friend of mine came to my house and walked into the room. After a short exchange and formalities I asked my friend if he would be willing to take a look at the initial pages of this book and tell me what he thought. He simply answered "No". While I was initially taken aback by his response I immediately thought back to my previous thoughts on hearing the word "No." I asked him why he didn't want to and he responded that he just didn't want to. It took me a moment to disperse my emotion. But after a deep breath I realized that he had his reasons for saying no. Maybe he didn't have time to read it, or perhaps he didn't like the pressure of critiquing my work. Regardless, I knew that there wasn't any false negative story behind it. He just said "no". Remember. Yes lives in a world of no. Get used to it.

6. Room Service Is For Losers

I travel and I travel a lot. I've gone months without seeing my own living room. When I travel, like most, I stay in hotels. When I stay in hotels I like to keep a motto in my head, "Room service is for losers." Don't take offense to that motto if you've ever indulged in some delicious and convenient food delivery. The reason I keep that motto in my mind is because it has led to some of the most exciting adventures I've experienced. When I stay in a hotel I know exactly what is going to happen if I order room service. I will make the call, they'll bring my order to the door, I'll sign the bill, and I'll remain in my room and finish the meal. On the other hand, if I decide to take action and leave the room, only God knows what will happen. I might meet the woman of my dreams; I might meet someone who will end up hiring me to do a presentation for them. Regardless, there is an unlived adventure at my fingertips.

This applies to your success as well. Think about all of the things in your mind that you want to accomplish. Maybe you want to get that raise you've been hoping for. Perhaps you want your artwork displayed in a certain gallery. Whatever your visions entail, they'll probably remain in the hotel room of your mind. Your thoughts need to leave the confines of your mind and make their way out into the adventurous world of the unknown. It's only in this unknown world that your ideas have the ability to become reality. Your ideas need room to grow. If you want that raise you should walk into your boss' office and ask him or her for the raise and tell him why you deserve it. If you want your artwork hung in that gallery you need to speak with the owner of the gallery and ask him or her if you can display your artwork there. It's the action that makes things happen. It's the Doing that makes you move forward. Room service is for losers.

7. Cynicism

The very title of this chapter goes against the nature of my being and against even the words I preach in this book. However, I wanted to give some short-lived attention to any people who, because of their nature, might not be able to grasp the power of this system. If you have led an analytical life you might not be able to believe the validity of this book.

The good friend of mine who wrote the email that inspired this book proposed an interesting question to me. He told me a story of his time spent in a poverty-stricken area of Ghana in Africa. He continued to describe meeting a man there who was born into poverty in a remote part of the world. After the story he simply asked "So, you're telling me that this guy can become an astronaut if he wants to?" And my answer was simply "Yes." His immediate response was "That's impossible!" While I can appreciate a realist's viewpoint, I had to retort. You see, it is quite "improbable" for a poor man in Africa to become an astronaut. However, it is not "impossible" Many people like my friend tend to lump the two together in an amalgamation. They are, in reality, two completely different things. It was also highly improbable that a small, lower class, underweight, and unacknowledged boy from a rural farming community in Pennsylvania would go on to achieve his dream and become the author of this book. Most people who I grew up with never thought in a million years that I would ever amount to anything. But using my mentality and system I was able to do it.

Nick and I continued to discuss the idea that anything is possible and debated the reality of the matter. We were sitting in the darkness of night on a hill in Muroran, Hokkaido in Japan overlooking a bay as we continued. I told him that if the man in Ghana had a truly heartfelt desire to become an astronaut, defined his goal, planned the actions to get there, and executed those actions, that he could do it. I did agree that it would be a long and difficult road filled with a lot of doable actions, but the fact remained that it was indeed possible. In explaining the possibility of this seemingly impossible goal, I was able to further my own understanding of what sets successful people apart from those that are doomed to failure. It was on top of that hill that I realized the power of thought.

In my opinion, the type of lens through which you view the world will determine the outcome of your life. It begins with what you choose to believe. Success and happiness are a choice. That's right, having success and happiness is a choice. It's a choice you make not once, but a choice you make every minute of your life. You are choosing how you see the world not in the moment, but as you're processing it. Your reaction to the world is a choice. If you choose to feel optimistic then you will lead an optimistic and happy life. If you choose to view the world through a lens of cynicism and skepticism, then you will live a life filled with all that comes with that viewpoint. Just as a cataract ruins the quality of your sight, so does the cataract of cynicism. Be positive and you will be positive. It's that simple.

"The only pessimist I can think of who was even remotely successful is Adolf Hitler. The only reason he was successful is because he ended up shooting himself."

-Wayne Hoffman

Here's a story to enlighten you: Once upon a time there was a girl who was born into poverty in rural Mississippi to a teenage single mother. Later in life she was raised in an inner city Milwaukee neighborhood. She experienced considerable hardship during her childhood. This unfortunate soul was raped and was molested by her cousin, her uncle, and a family friend, starting when she was nine years old and became pregnant at 14; her son died in infancy. She was then sent to live with the man she calls her father in Tennessee. Her mother was a housemaid. The girl had believed that her biological father was a coal miner turned barber. Her half-brother died of AIDS.

At 13, after suffering years of abuse, she ran away from home. However, just like the man in Ghana who has the potential to be an astronaut, the girl in this story also had potential. Despite her position in the world, she chose to view the world through a positive lens and went on to become the woman we know as Oprah Winfrey. As of the print date of this book she has a net worth over $2.7 billion and currently holds the title of "Richest self-made woman in America."

Feel. Define. Plan. Do.

"Everyone wants to be rich and famous. But how many of them are making an active effort to achieve it?"

-Wayne Hoffman

8. Your Funeral

A rather morbid title to a chapter isn't it? This is another interesting exercise that I learned somewhere along the way. Hopefully I can recall where I learned it before this book goes to print. This is one of the more interesting experiments that I've tried. It had a profound effect on me the first time I tried it and I'm sure it will do the same for you. Here it is in a nutshell. Imagine your funeral. (If you plan on being cremated or living forever this exercise still applies to you.) Imagine you're at your own funeral. Imagine you look inside the coffin and see yourself. Now look around. Who is there? What faces can you pick out of the crowd? Now imagine that all of those people, one by one, stands up and says something about you. What would you want each person to say about you? Imagine your friends, business partners, family, old classmates, the stranger from the coffee shop, your mechanic, your mailman, and all the people you interact with on a daily or yearly basis. Hear the words that come out of their mouths.

After you've done this take a look at your goals and vision of the future. Do their words match up with your goals? Keep the baseline important things in mind while constructing your future. Sure, it might be nice to own a Ferrari and be a millionaire. But did you help others? Were you kind to your friends and family? Having a deep-rooted sense of what is truly important is a wonderful ally in your journey toward creating the ultimate you.

Addendum

It is December 5th, 2011 and I'm currently on a ship sailing through Indonesia on my way to Bali. On this journey I began reading a book that was recommended to me by a colleague. The book, which I highly recommend, is entitled The 7 Habits of Highly Effective People by Stephen R. Covey. I found it interesting that he had the same exact "funeral" exercise is in his book as well. I wanted to note that fact and give him a friendly nod and a smile. Either great minds think alike or great principles and ideas are universal.

9. Why?

Most people move along their journey asking the question "What?". What can I do to make money? What should I do for a living? What should I do with the money I make? They also like the question "Who?" Who will I marry? Who are my true friends? However, most people neglect the most important question of them all. That question is "Why?"

Asking yourself why you are doing something will help you reach true clarity and define what the world means to you. It will help you find your place in the universe. Did you ever have a feeling of being lost in your life…not sure where to go or what to do? The simple act of asking yourself "why" is the first step in moving toward your destiny. A direct example is the book you're currently reading. Why did I write this book? I wrote it because I want to help people. I find a great sense of happiness and inner peace knowing that the words on these pages will have a positive effect on someone's life. If this information is properly conveyed, then it will have a positive effect on not only you, but the people you may choose to share these ideas with.

Why do you work the job you're working? Put aside the answer "Because I need money to pay bills." If you're currently unemployed then ask yourself why you will be working for your future job. Truly think about the contribution you're making toward fulfilling your own definition of life. This is heavy stuff isn't it? People always ask the age-old question "What is the meaning of life?" I am about to tell you the answer: The meaning of life is subjective. Meaning, the answer is different for everyone. YOU decide the meaning of life. The meaning isn't something you look for, it's something that comes from within yourself. Your purpose and meaning is completely different from everyone else. The trick is to define that meaning and do action steps that create movement toward fulfilling your definition. It's creating intent.

Now is the time to cut through all the bullshit and figure out the true meaning of YOUR life. You decide.

10. Start being a laser beam.

Many people take all of their energy and use it to inch forward in many different areas of their lives. They get a sense of achievement from tiny details that when added up don't advance their lives at all. Let me clarify that unnecessary actions are much different than the very important "Next doable actions" that I described earlier. Many of you may work in an office setting. If you do, then a great analogy I can use is to compare the unnecessary actions to it's cousin "busy work" You know, the kind of work that you do when nobody is looking. Organizing paperclips, stacking your business cards on your desk so they look neat, watering the office plants, typing a lengthy email when a five second phone could have been made instead. You know, busy work. This type of mentality can kill a person's dreams in the slowest, most torturous way. If you allow this type of action into your life your dreams should start writing their last will and testament. I highly recommend focusing your energy on particular goals and doing meaningful actions that will help you achieve them. The trick is to prioritize your goals and attack the first one on your list with all your heart.

Imagine the energy that you put into a project is like the light from a light bulb. It's spread across the whole room and doesn't highlight any part of the room. How many lights have you turned off and on today? It would probably take you a minute to think about it. The reason you don't remember is because it wasn't tremendously noteworthy or important. Now compare your energy to the light that is emitted from a laser beam. A laser beam is an impressive light that directly affects one particular spot in the room and is very memorable. The light from a laser beam is focused and tremendously powerful. You would definitely remember seeing a laser beam shooting across the room.

The same way a laser is powerful and impressive, so should be the energy that you put into the various projects in your life. Give each individual project the attention it deserves. Make sure you prioritize. Don't put energy into a project that doesn't deserve it. What's important to you? If it's important, make it important. If it's not important, get rid of it.

11. Come *from* your goals.

A lot of people ask me how they can reach their goals. One of the first things I like to point out to them is that you shouldn't move toward your goals but come *from* your goals. Let me explain. If you want to become the number one in your line of work, then *be* the number one in your line of work. Ask yourself, how would the person at the top act, walk, talk, communicate? Once you figure that out, then proceed to do just that.

I had a close friend who works as a model approach me about coaching her. She told me she wanted to be the number one model in the world and do ads for Gucci and Prada, etc. Shortly thereafter she created a biography for her newly established website. When I read through the bio it read something like this: "I'm just a small town girl with big dreams. I'm trying to make it as a model and I hope I can do it." Those weren't her exact words, but you get the point. I asked her what the number one model in the world would put as her bio. Would she describe herself in that way? No. So, I instantly advised her to change her bio to one that represented who she wanted to be. Not to be untruthful of course, but to come *from* her goals. I told her to be the person she wants to be rather than try to become it.

If you begin to truly *be* the person you envision yourself becoming, you instantly become that person. It's a quite simple concept that eludes most people. It's almost incomprehensible to think that you can just instantly become the person you want to be. But it's just that simple. Remember our rock star? If he believes that he is the number one rock star in the world and effectively communicates that to the rest of the world, then he becomes just that. If he comes from his goal then he is already at the finish line. Now the rest of the world needs to catch up. He can stay still and let the world come to him. Be the best. Know you're the best. Come *from* your goals.

P.S

The model I just told you about just signed with the number modeling agency in the world and just signed a contract to do an ad for Gucci. It IS possible.

12. You Can't Do It Alone

Don't argue. You can't. Look at all the people you deem successful. They are not a one-man show. Every person who ever achieved success has had a team of people who supported him or her physically, emotionally, spiritually, or all of the above. Does the president run the country by himself? No, he has thousands of people who help him on a daily basis. Do Olympic athletes train by themselves? No, they have a team of physical therapists and coaches helping them. Are governments truly run by one person? No. So begin to realize that you have to start building a dream team that believes in you just as much as you do.

Building your team is not an easy task. It's not something you can do overnight. However, you can take the first steps toward finding the people or at least the type of people you want to surround yourself with.

"Birds of a feather flock together."

-Unknown

Take a good look at the people you are surrounding yourself with right now. Do they represent the type of success and happiness that you would like to obtain? Most of us can identify those that do while at the same time we can identify those that absolutely do not. I highly recommend taking a good look at your circle of friends and business partners and choose to hang out with the people who make you a better person and whom you have the will to help become better. There are probably a handful of people who you can identify as being individuals who have achieved some level of success personally, spiritually, or in business. Take the time to nurture those relationships.

Make sure you ask yourself what you are bringing to the table as well. It's a common mistake for people to enter into a relationship with a very selfish attitude. People often subconsciously ask themselves what they're going to get out of the interaction. A more important question to ponder is what you are giving. I have found throughout my life that people receive the most from relationships that they put a lot into. Now don't get me wrong, I've experienced a few instances, as I'm sure you may have, where you give your heart and soul to nurturing a business or romantic relationship and your efforts are not rewarded or recognized at all. Keep those negative experiences out of your mind and remember that we all receive through giving. I'm not sure if you believe in karma, but it's a natural human instinct to help those that help us.

Let's take for example your local bar. On any given weekend you can be sure to find a man who will inevitably offer to buy a girl a drink. There are two main reasons for this. The one we'll focus on is the fact that the girl, possibly, will feel an obligation to the stranger to at least engage in small talk. This leaves an open door for our imaginary man to strike up a conversation and possibly find a suitable mate.

It's in this primal part of the brain where giving makes us want to reciprocate any display of help or selflessness. Did a friend of yours ever pay for dinner? If so, you may have immediately responded "Thanks, I'll get the next one." Keep this idea in the forefront of your mind as you interact with potential members of your dream team. If you have something to offer them, they will more likely find things to offer you. Give, and give generously.

Remember to take your goals into consideration when forming your team. Write down a list of things that, when you're at the pinnacle of your success, you'll need help with. It's the things you need help with now and the things you will one day need help with that will be the basis of forming your support team. One area to consider is your romantic endeavors. Is the person you are with right now or will be with one day able to offer the kind of support you need to succeed? I'm not a relationship counselor by any means, but if you answered "No", I would rethink your choice of mate. I feel it's almost impossible to succeed unless the person/people you interact with on a daily basis are behind you one hundred percent. I've seen too many people's dreams crushed because they're family, friends, or spouse didn't believe in their potential. You can either swim upstream or replace the river.

You have a choice of the people you surround yourself with. The only exception to that is your family. We are born into our family or placed into foster care from the start. When dealing with family you must take a proactive stance to gain their trust in your goals and make them see your vision. In some cases your family will not agree with your passions and will be the farthest thing from a dream team. But after you succeed, I guarantee they will applaud you, even if only in their own minds.

13. Under Pressure

"Break the pressure. Come play my game, I'll test you."

Musician: Prodigy Song: Mindfields

One of the most difficult things to endure is the constant pressure of people telling you that you can't achieve something. How many times have you heard a friend or family member tell you that you should give up? I'm sure you've heard it at least once. These words are one of the most damaging things a person can hear. This section of the book is a very important one and I don't want you to take it lightly. This section may very well determine your fate. So please read it slowly and carefully.

Although I have come to a level of great success, there is one thing that I must do on a constant basis. That thing is fighting the negative thoughts of others, as well as, negative thoughts that form in my own mind. The true test of whether you will become successful is in whether or not you can constantly and consistently fight through those words. To put it in perspective I will share a short story with you. When I was a kid I wanted to become a magician. To my father I might as well have wanted to become a unicorn that could breath fire. My father lovingly said "Wayne, how many magicians are there in the world?" "Tens of thousands or more" I answered. He then responded, "That's right. And how many of them have become successful and made it onto television?" I pondered the question for an absurdly long time before I said, "David Copperfield did." That's all I could think of. My father's final response was " That's right. You have a one-in-a-million shot of becoming successful. You should get a job with a bank instead."

He was right. The chances of me making it were slim-to-none. His words ripped my dreams apart. Nine out of ten people would have listened to my father and taken a job offer at a bank instead. There was something that I did differently however. I didn't listen to him. Instead I continued performing with full intent to make it. A few years later I was touring the world and landed a spot on primetime national television. I was on live television…in front of millions of people. I made it.

During the years between that conversation and my inevitable success I was faced with the formidable years of high school. (Add groans here) Those years were both helpful and hurtful at the same time. Although the excitement and smiles I got from casually performing in school were great, there were a few people who thought I was a lunatic. I still remember one classmate who once said, "So you're going to be a magician for a living? Hahahahaha. What a joke. Are you serious? You can't make money from that." I wanted to punch him in the face at that time. Again, most people would have let that demolish their dreams. But I didn't. I had such passion for what I do that I kept fighting through everyone's negativity. I was able to brush it off.

On a side note: that same individual is now my biggest fan and constantly emails me asking me about my life and he continues to tell me how he wishes he was in my shoes. And yes, I get a small sense of satisfaction from it. It's horrible but true. (I have a slightly devilish grin on my face right now)

It's important to note that you *will* have people who are going to try to stop you from reaching your goals. It's not a matter of whether or not it will happen. It's a matter of when. They may try to do it physically, but more than likely it will be a psychological attack. I want you to prepare for it. It's on this psychological battleground that you will either win your war or perish at the hands of pessimism and negativity. You have to train yourself to accept that there are negative people and learn to brush off their comments. I like to call these negative feelings you get from outside influence "The Ocean of Emotion." Make sure you know how to swim.

Here's another great example of determination of a politician from the mid 1800's:

1832: Lost his job. Defeated for state legislature.

1833: Failed in business.

1835: His sweetheart died.

1836: Had a nervous breakdown.

1838: Defeated for speaker.

1843: Defeated for nomination for Congress.

1848: Lost re-nomination.

1849: Rejected for land officer.

1854: Defeated for US Senate.

1856: Defeated for nomination for Vice President.

1858: Again defeated for US Senate.

After all of these negative things happening to him this man kept trying. He kept ignoring people's rejections of him. He didn't care what people thought of him and he brushed off the negativity. In 1860, two years after his final defeat in his bid for the US Senate, he was elected President of the United States of America. His name was Abraham Lincoln. The point here is to continue to fight for what you want. This is where the first step in the Hoffman System becomes so extremely important. You must *feel* the intense desire for what you want. It's during these turbulent emotional times when it becomes not only important, but also essential.

I have a theory on why so many people try to stop others from achieving success. It stems from two different things. The first is that most people have a very narrow view of the world. They grow up looking at the people that surround them and use them as indicators for what is possible in the world. That's not a bad thing. It's just the way things are. Most of the naysayers that are of the same age as you will probably come from this train of thought. The other thought path comes from people who are older than you and have not achieved much success in their own lives. They will undoubtedly hold the small subconscious thought that if you succeed, then they themselves never lived up to their full potential. Can you imagine the uncomfortable feeling someone would have if they realize that they wasted their entire life? It would be devastating. Your success could bring that feeling into their lives. So it seems they would much rather have you follow the same path that they themselves walked.

Don't listen to them. Rather, don't give what they say any credibility. You will not have a choice on whether or not you listen to them. They will surely find a way to cram their negative beliefs into your life. Create a pact with yourself to not let it bother you, and if it does begin to bother you, then you have to have a plan on how you're going to deal with it. Again, this is where your support team comes into play. Be prepared and have someone you can talk to.

Another area of turmoil you need to prepare for is that of the real world, aka Murphy's Law. Murphy's Law states "Anything that can go wrong, will go wrong." If you plan on being successful you have to plan on failing. One of the hardest things to deal with while attempting to reach a goal is any type of failure. Many people will go through a rough time or two and give up. They give up not because they can't handle it, but because they didn't have a plan for when they hit failure. How many times in your life have you said, "I can't take it, I just can't handle this anymore"? The fact of the matter is, you *were* able to handle it. You are just fine. Whatever you said you couldn't handle is obviously in your past. You did it. Congratulations.

Now start thinking about your goals and the things that might get in your way. You might not have enough money. You might injure yourself. Whatever your goal is, realize that there will be setbacks. Just make sure you create a doable plan to deal with them. But remember; don't spend too much time dwelling on negative thoughts. Spend as much time as it takes to understand possible roadblocks and create a plan. After that, go right back to envisioning the positive things that lie in your future.

Remember that success is much like weight training. It's not as easy as staring at your muscles and they grow. No, you have to work. There are periods of strain and periods of rest. There is a constant state of flux. Your attempts and inevitable triumph at success will have the same flux.

"Get knocked down seven times. Get up eight"

-Ancient Chinese Proverb

14. Check Yourself Before You Wreck Yourself

Let's take a moment to give your mind a break. If you've been reading non-stop since page one you've probably tried to cram a lot of information in to your brain. At this point you may be excited at the vision of your future. Well, at least I hope so. But I won't make any assumptions. I hate when authors do that in books. Let's at least assume you've read everything up until this point and didn't just skip ahead to this sentence. Take a moment to evaluate how you feel. Do you feel like you've moved forward as a person? Make sure you take the time to read through this book more than once. Every idea in these pages isn't something you learn once and it instantly sticks with you. More than likely your mind will want to go back to it's old ways and force you into your old routine.

Treat this book like you would if you were forgiving yourself. Please, let me elaborate. Forgiveness is not something that you do once. Forgiveness is a thing you do on a daily basis. It's not saying you won't feel upset anymore.

It's recognizing that you *will* feel upset and won't let it affect your thoughts and actions.

Use this same mentality when wielding the information in this book. Reread the book often to refresh your mind and your spirit. Every mind needs to recharge just like the body. Consider this book food for your mind and spirit. In fact, consider it *Mind Candy*. In fact, it's as I write this sentence that I think I just came up with a great title for this project. I hadn't thought of a title until now, I've just been saving it on my computer as "My Book".

It's always a good idea to schedule report card moments in your life. Scheduling specific dates on your calendar that force you to review your progress is an extremely helpful tool. In fact, take a moment to put "Create a Mind Candy report card" on your calendar. Choose a date about 6 months from now. When you begin to analyze your progress six months from now you will surely have two reactions. One will be a sense of satisfaction, and the other will be a sadness that you didn't work hard enough. Don't worry. It happens to the best of us. But the latter of those two reactions is the exact reason behind having a report card moment. It gives you time to reflect on your progress from an almost objective view. Make sure you ask yourself specific questions about your goals and grade yourself using any scale you'd like, number or letter. Hopefully we see more A-pluses and one hundred percent's than we see F's or zeros.

I like to use the report card idea in every area of my life. One of the most helpful things in my romantic relationships has been using the report card moment. I ask the girl in our relationship to grade me on different areas and then explain her grade. The key to having a successful and fruitful outcome is to ensure her complete immunity from whatever she says. In other words, I can't get upset if she says something negative. I do these report card moments when my mind and heart is completely clear. You can't have a report card moment if you're in an emotional state. You have to be able to look at everything objectively.

It's in these amazing moments when I can find out exactly how she feels. You would be surprised about the level of honesty one provides when they feel secure and safe. If you grade yourself on levels of success in other areas of your life make sure you grant yourself the same courtesy. Be honest with yourself. Allow yourself to truly analyze your progress with an almost perfectly objective view. Did you do what you said you were going to do? If not, why? Learning to objectively rate your progress will ensure your success. It worked throughout your childhood. The teacher gave you a report card and you probably took it home to show your parents. This time you play the roll of the child and the parent. You can do it. I have faith in you.

15. A Request From The Author

Please do me a favor. If you feel like you have received something valuable from this book, tell three people about it. You'll be indirectly thanking me while at the same time helping three people that you feel could benefit from it. You could probably think of three people right now that could gain something from these ideas. If you feel so inclined, tell more than three. It is my goal to share this information with the rest of the world. I'd love to sell one million copies of the book before I die. That is the goal that I have defined in my mind but I need your help to do it. You are part of my dream team. I think that if everyone had these tools in their hand that they could lead the happy and productive life they deserve. Give, and give generously.

16. Here's a big one for you

Think big. You're not thinking big enough. Take your vision and take it to the extreme. If you want something make sure you want the whole thing. A lot of people think of the next doable action but they don't take it to the ultimate doable action. I like stories, so let me regale you. Many years ago I was friends with a magician who, like me, had dreams of making it big. I used to hear stories of how he wanted to go on the local public access channel and do a show for the local audience. Although it was more ambitious than most I now realize that the idea he had was probably not the ultimate level of success that he imagined.

Although being on television in any capacity is a great achievement, he failed to look beyond the easy outlet of local television and see the possibility of national or international exposure. At the time I was in the same shoes, unable to look into the sky and see the big picture. What were we really trying to accomplish? Did we want to make it semi-big or did we want to make it big? It was then that I told my manager to call the Ellen DeGeneres Show and make them have me as a guest. His initial reaction was quite expected. "How the hell am I supposed to do that?" he asked. I told him a theory that until this day holds major significance in the story of my success. For those of you who live outside of the United States or who are not familiar with the show, The Ellen DeGeneres Show is a well-known daytime talk show that has a very large viewership and fan base.

The theory is quite simple; think big. This is an idea that has made my career explode in leaps and bounds. In fact, all but one of my TV appearances has stemmed from using this mentality. I told my manager that there is a person whose main job is to book guests for the Ellen DeGeneres Show. That same person has a telephone, eats, sleeps, goes to the bathroom, and farts. All you have to do is figure out whom that person is and let them know that I exist. After that, it's in fate's hands.

His first phone call was to NBC corporate office. When the secretary answered he quite simply said, "Hello, I'd like to get my artist on the Ellen DeGeneres Show, could you tell me whom I would need to speak to in order to make that happen?" The secretary told him that he needed to contact the producers of the show. His next question was "Can you tell me their name and give me their phone number?" After a series of similar phone calls he dialed one last time. This time he received an answering machine message that said something to the effect of, "Thanks for calling the talent coordinator for the Ellen DeGeneres Show. Please leave your name and number after the beep."

A short time after leaving a message he received a return call. After that, I was on the show. It was that simple. Using a very simple humanistic mentality combined with a think-big frame of mind, we were able to create the impossible. Many people want to be on television, but very few take the actions needed to end up there. After my manager realized the power of thinking big and thinking simply, we were on fire. Shortly after my initial TV appearances, they kept coming. All you have to do is think about the ultimate level of success that you want to obtain and go for exactly that. You can't make excuses like "Well, if I want to be on TV I have to start small and work my way up." Why? No you don't.

If you start small then you start small. Think about it. Why not start big? There is no rule. The world likes to trick you into thinking that there are rules that govern your life. These imaginary rules are passed down from generation to generation with no grounds to support their validity. Why do you have to start small and work your way up? The truth is, you don't. Go for want you want like a dart player shoots for the bulls-eye. You may not hit the bulls-eye on your first throw. But if you keep aiming for what you want, you will eventually hit it. When you play darts you don't say, "Well, I'll aim for a lower number and work my way to the bulls-eye" nor do you say "I'll try to hit one pin and work my way up to a strike" when bowling. Why are you making an exception in other areas of your life?

One of the funny things I can remember from my adventures was the day I told my manager to call Donald Trump and tell him that I wanted to wager one million dollars on a single hand of blackjack in one of his casinos and televise it. The look on my manager's face was similar to when I told him I wanted to be on the Ellen DeGeneres Show. It was the look of "How the hell am I supposed to do that?" This time, however, he knew exactly what to do. His first call was to the lobby of the Trump Tower in New York City. When the receptionist answered my manager calmly and seriously asked,

"Can I please speak to Mr. Donald Trump?" The receptionist probably wondered whether it was a prank call.

After an awkward moment the receptionist told my manager that they couldn't connect him with Mr. Trump. My manager, ever so seriously asked, "Who is the highest ranking person you can connect me with?" Shortly thereafter he was connected with the manager of the building, the head of marketing & public relations, and so on. Finally my manager spoke with Donald Trump's right-hand man. He was only one step away from speaking to Donald Trump himself. How did he do it? He used the advise from one of Donald's books. He was thinking big.

Do yourself a favor and reevaluate your next doable actions. Are they leading you toward your real goal or they only leading you up a small step? Think big. Imagine you are the most powerful person in the world and imagine you have unlimited money. What would you do? Go toward that vision rather than being satisfied with a watered down version of what you really want. Go get the real deal.

17. Tick Tock

I want you to think back to your time in school. It could be college, high school, or elementary school. For some of you it will be like imagining yesterday, literally. While some of you may have to go back a few years…or decades. Regardless of how long ago it was, I want you to think back to when your teacher gave you a project to complete. When they assigned the project they no doubt gave you a date that the project was due. In other words, they gave you a deadline. Do you remember when you and most of your classmates finished the project? That's right, the night before it was due. You stayed up all night, drank a caffeinated beverage, and crammed until you passed out. But you probably got it finished in time and gained a sense of accomplishment from it.

Now let's look at how that scenario affects your daily life right now. A simple human rule exists: Work expands to fill the time up until it's deadline. We all procrastinate. Well, at least most of us. We all take care of things when they are a necessity and take the path of least resistance. I mean, who wants to work? Nobody. However, it can cause a problem when that work goes on forever due to a lack of a deadline. The point here is to set due dates for all of your projects. No matter how big or small, all of your goals must have a time to be completed.

Let's say for example that you have a goal to paint your house. Every time you come home from work you will look at the chipping paint and say to yourself "I have to paint the house" This will continue every day and cause you stress. The way to alleviate the stress is to actually schedule a day to paint the house and/or have the house painted. In other words, create a deadline or a "due date". This had to be recorded on a calendar so that you are accountable for it. Then you can prepare by buying paint and brushes, paint the house on the scheduled day, and complete your project by it's expiration date. How many of you know someone who always says "I'll get around to it" but never actually gets anything done? Don't be one of those people. Schedule specific days to complete tasks.

You can also apply this thinking to other, more pleasurable areas of your life. Let's say taking a vacation. I know a lot of people who comment on the amount of traveling that I do. Many of them always tell me that one-day they want to come with me on one of my trips. The problem is I'm currently sitting in a hotel room and I just finished mapping out my next journey, which includes Vietnam, Bali, Australia, and Hawaii. I'll point out that nobody is coming with me. The reason being that nobody put it on their calendar to join me for the adventures. People like to talk the talk but never...well, you know. And I figured out why. Keep reading.

I just read a study that found that talking about goals creates the same sense of accomplishment in the brain as actually completing the goal. So by telling someone that you plan to climb Mount Everest you are getting the same feeling as actually climbing it. It reminds me of all the people in Hollywood who are going to make the next big blockbuster movie. The thing to realize is that you can talk all you want, but you have to actually DO the tasks that create the end result. In a nutshell: Create deadlines for all the projects in your head. Create the deadlines right now.

18. Earplugs

Did you ever notice that the most successful people in any particular field often got their start at a young age? Many people would attribute their success to many years of practice or education in their field. However, I believe that isn't the true catalyst to their success. Sure, practicing and studying will give you the skills required to be proficient at a certain career, but there is something instilled in all of them that is the true reason for their success. They have earplugs.

I don't mean earplugs in the literal sense. I am referring to their natural ability to disregard the statements of others. Most people who followed their true passion found the words of the people around them meaningless. Their desire to follow their hearts desire outweighed anything else. You probably know someone who, as a child, probably wanted to do something completely different than what they are doing now. Over time, other people's words may have influenced them to follow a different path. Perhaps that person is you.

There are a select few who, despite people pushing their opinions on them, were able to tune out the words of everyone around them and follow their dreams. You too can have this ability. All you have to do is practice. Imagine that right now I hand you a set of earplugs. Actually imagine you reach out and grab them. Picture them in your favorite color. Imagine you put them in your ears and in that moment all sound stops. You can't hear the people telling you that your dreams are impossible. You can't hear the imaginary reasons why your ideas are insane. Right now in this moment, you have no thoughts other than your own.

The thing you should learn is that you can't block the sound of people's opinions on your ears; however, you can decide how you filter those sounds out once they reach your brain. Everyday we are influenced to believe certain things. Trillions of dollars are spent every year on advertising that tries to make you purchase certain products. Radio ads, television ads, ads on websites, billboards, even bumper stickers. Look around right now. You can probably see several logos on things you've purchased. If you can't see the logos you might be able to see something you bought. Look at your clothes.

Are you wearing a particular brand that you like? Then their advertising worked.

In order to succeed at making your dreams a reality, you must learn the masterful art of not listening to others. Those who started pursuing their passion at a young age most likely had the natural ability to decrease the value in other people's negative words. Either that, or didn't have anyone feeding them negative thoughts. You have to realize that during your life you will interact with thousands of people who have their own agendas, thoughts, opinions, and feelings. The second thing you need to realize is that you have the ability to choose how you react to them. You and you alone are the one who can decide the value in the things you hear and read.

Often times the people who love us most are the ones who hold us back from reaching our dreams. Our parents are often the people who pass judgment on our decisions, and because we value their opinion, we listen to them. In that moment we lose the very thing they wanted to give us: happy and fulfilling lives. But it's not too late. In this very moment you have an amazing ability. You have the power to choose. Many people live as victims. They choose to live their lives as victims of an imaginary circumstance. People love to create stories that keep them in what I like to call "comfortable discomfort"

It's easy for us to blame others for the position we're currently in. We can say things like "I can't do it because the economy isn't good right now", or "I don't have enough money to reach my goal." The funny thing about these false stories is that they aren't end-all statements. The only statement that you could say that is a viable excuse is the one thing you can never say and mean: "I am dead"

The only question you have to ask yourself is "How?" You can ask yourself "In this current economy, HOW can I succeed?" and "I don't have enough money, so HOW can I earn it so that I can do what I want?" I guarantee you there is always an answer. But there is a catch. Even though there is an answer, often times the people around you will convince you that there is not. That's when you have to put your mental earplugs in. You have to listen to what they say, ask yourself why they would say those things, and then process their words. Did they say those things because they have a limited view of the world? Did they say those things because they want to protect you from possible failure?

The difficult part of tuning out the words of people telling you that you can't succeed is that the words are often mixed with emotion. The emotion comes from the person speaking the words and in turn emotionally affects you. Imagine you had your earplugs in and you couldn't hear them. What would you think then? What actions would you take? Those are the things that matter most. Those are the things that will lead you to your destiny.

19. Your Feet

As I was sailing on a cruise ship somewhere in the Caribbean I kicked back to relax in my cabin after a long day. When I turned on the TV I saw several men facing death as they scaled the infamous Hilary Step on Mount Everest. At this last, and critical part of their monumental climb, one of the climbers said something that stuck with me: "Never look past your feet."

To the left and the right side of this guy was a one-mile plunge into a cold abyss. If you take one wrong step you could plummet to your death. His point was a good one. No matter how large your goal may be, you must not look past your feet. Another excellent quote I read that summarizes this theory is "Keep your hands in the world and your mind on the infinite."

Although you have to think big when it comes to your end goal, you have to make sure you look at where your feet are at this exact moment. In other words, focus on what are you doing right now. Are you being efficient in your work and moving forward or are you taking steps that might make you plummet into the abyss of non-success? Many times we are so overzealous that we forget to feel our own breath.

As you're reading this sentence I want you to take a deep breath inward and feel it fill your lungs. As you exhale feel the sensation of the air leaving your body. Try it now. Think about the importance of that single function. Without it you would not be alive. Yet, we often forget about those little things that keep us going. We focus our energy on the many unimportant distractions and we think about the big picture too much. Although it's crucial to have a large clear picture of what you are trying to accomplish, remember that you cannot look past your feet. If you forget to watch the little steps, you might destroy everything you're trying to achieve.

This goes back to asking yourself what the next doable action is in your plan. I'm sure you've heard the popular phrase "A journey of a thousand miles begins with the first step." This is truer than you can imagine. Although some of these quotes sound like something you would find in a fortune cookie, they are indeed real. They are so real that your acknowledgement of them will determine your fate.

Sometimes your feet hurt. Sometimes you don't want to even take one more step. Be it mentally or physically. The fine line that separates those that are successful and those that are not is the not-so-simple ability to push forward through mental and physical restraints. Do your feet hurt? Are you committed to take another step although you don't feel like it? If you are committed, you will succeed. I guarantee it. Evidence of this can be seen in the words you're reading right now. I'm sitting in an airport (as usual) and I'm quite exhausted. Last night I was in Pennsylvania and performed a show, I then fulfilled a commitment to attend a party to celebrate my friend's birthday, after that I packed my things and went straight to the airport to board a flight. I am now two flights into my day and waiting to board a third. I've been awake for 30-some hours and one of the main things on my mind is obviously sleep. However, I made a commitment to use my free time to add more thoughts and theories into this book. My "feet" hurt, but I'm still taking steps. This book is being written using the principles in this section. Without them I would be no farther along with completing this book than I was when I first started typing it. Use that same push in your own life and you will see amazing things begin to happen.

Feel your breath. Watch your steps.

20. When Passion Meets Luck Meets Work

I recently realized that if you combine a passion, a little luck, and some work you could create something powerful. This shows that your passions will inevitably show their face in your life whether you like it or not. I always urge people to follow their passions regardless of what imaginary story they find themselves living in. I came to this conclusion by chance while I was digging through the applications on my computer. I stumbled upon an application I used to create what's known as a "look book" for my commercial agent. The program allows you to import photos and align them in order to print a book. What I didn't realize at the time was that the program was much more advanced than I first thought. It allowed the user to create an entire book with backgrounds, frames, and other editing attributes. I immediately uploaded about fifty photos that I had taken from my travels around the world and began creating a book of my photos. Two days later I'm still working on the book and will soon be finished. After I'm finished I will be sending the files to a printer to be printed.

The end result, a book, was created in a matter of days because of my passion for photography. I always love taking photos of the interesting things I see in daily life. Some of these things include sunsets over the Caribbean, rice fields in Bali, nightclubs in Vegas, or glaciers in Alaska. Capturing these moments brings me great joy and immediately my passion revealed itself when I found out that I had the capability to bring those photos into the hands of the public. If you're passionate about something, whether it's sports, movies, computers, cooking or otherwise, make time to do it. If you are really adventurous you might even be able to monetize your passion. In other words, make money from something you enjoy. I'm planning on selling my book of photos to my fans. Who knows…someone might even buy one.

Analyze your life right now. Look at the things you enjoy. Not necessarily the things that come to mind right away, but think about the things you would do if you didn't have to work. People often put most of these things on the back burner. The sad part about that lies in the fact that those things are what life is truly about. Some people may argue that fact, however, it's impossible to argue that things that make you happy aren't important. If you take a look at the things you enjoy, you can most certainly make time to not only do more of them, but also possibly even profit from them. Follow your passion, stir in a little luck, and a dash of work, and you have a recipe for a happy and prosperous life.

21. Feeling Lucky?

Are you a lucky person? Do you find that things always seem to fall into place? I do. However, I've noticed that people who tell me that they are unlucky seem to have that exact fate. My personal belief is that those who feel that they are lucky will find themselves enjoy life and noticing the good in everything. On the contrary, those who feel that they are doomed to an unlucky life will always tend to focus their minds on the small, normally insignificant things that happen throughout life. If you begin to pick out the negative things that happen in life you will only notice those things. In return, your thoughts of negativity will breed an unhealthy environment that will stunt your growth as an individual.

Most of the time we react to external stimulus without thinking of the truth behind the experience. We will often tell a tale of a horrible day filled with stressing and seemingly unlucky circumstances. The truth of the matter is that you're just fine at the end of the day. It's your choice as to whether or not those circumstances continue to bother you throughout your week. The only thing you need to ask yourself is "What is the next doable action I can take to feel better?" The answer will always be there. You just have to put aside any emotion that may be attached to the situation and do the action that you decided on. To set aside emotions is stereotypically a male trait, however both men and women can learn to train themselves to look at life through a lens of objectivity.

If I told you that you could live longer through a simple yes or no choice, would you want to know what that choice was? Of course! It's a proven scientific fact that those who lead a stress-free lifestyle live longer. If you choose to check your emotions at the door, you have in your hands a proverbial fountain of youth. A simple technique that I created is asking myself a simple question…

"Will this matter a year from now?"

If the answer to the question is no, then you should make an agreement with yourself to let the experience go. It's a innate human experience to create false stories as to why the small insignificant tribulations you might have is "the worst experience EVER" The reality remains that negative thing consuming your mind is probably not that significant. The key to checking your emotions is to analyze why you feel the way you do and create a plan that you can execute in order to feel better. Often times the plan will be as simple as saying "I agree to let it go" Remember that phrase. It will serve you well.

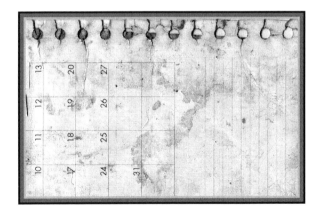

22. Stop Being A Crybaby

When we are born we are at the mercy of the world. It is because of the people who raised us that we are alive. Without them, we wouldn't be here. When we are babies we have a very simple system of communicating our needs. We cry. If a baby is hungry, the baby cries and someone comes and feeds them. If the baby has a dirty diaper, they cry and someone changes them. It's a simple system but it works. However, there is something that happens during that process that sticks with us into adulthood. We learn that satisfaction and happiness comes from an outside source. We learn that in order to be happy, someone else needs to provide it to us either through words or actions. The unfortunate part about that experience is when you become an adult you continue using that flawed model. When you get to the point where you can feed, clothe, and shelter yourself, (aka adulthood), you should also be able to maintain your own happiness. AS we go through life we often look for other people's approval to signify our self-worth. The truth of the matter is this: Happiness comes from within. It is self-actualized. Happiness no longer comes from an outside source. Happiness is quite simply a choice.

I know, I know…it's hard to digest. All these years you've been blaming other people for your unhappiness. In actuality you had the power to be happy the entire time. If you're a movie buff then you can instantly relate this idea to one of the most famous movies in cinematic history, The Wizard of Oz. If you haven't seen the movie then put this book down. We are no longer friends. All joking aside, it perfectly illustrates my point. As you might be able to recall, in the movie Dorothy, the main character, is lost in an imaginary world of a talking scarecrow, a cowardly lion, a tin man, and other characters. She is lost in a crazy world and desires to go to the happiness and safety of her home. Throughout the movie she searches for the answer to her happiness and seeks it from others. In the end she learns that she held the power to go home the entire time. All she had to do was close her eyes, click her heels three times, and say the words "There's no place like home"

I'm here to tell you that you also have the power to obtain happiness. You need to stop looking to the characters in your life to get it. All you have to do is close your eyes, feel your own breath, and say the words "I choose to be happy." In that moment, despite anything that is going on in your life, you create happiness. I personally choose happiness all the time. In my world I'm faced with what to most people are stressful and horrible issues such as delayed and cancelled flights, problems with employees, family issues, and other not-so-pleasant times. However, instead of letting the outside negativity decide my emotions, I CHOOSE to be happy.

Negativity will always exist. It is part of a universal and ever-present balance of life. There will be birth and there will be death. There will be a sunrise and a sunset. The key to leading a happy life is in the way you react to the things that come into your life. Here's a story that will help explain my idea: About two months prior to the time that I'm typing this I was relaxing on a cruise ship in the Caribbean. I finished a performance on a ship and was enjoying the sunshine. I had planned on staying in Aruba for a few days following my performance on the ship. I got an email from my agent who told me he booked me a performance in Cedar Falls, Iowa. Although I was enjoying the sunshine I was also excited to perform for another group of excited soon-to-be fans. The next day arrived and I planned my day: Fly to Miami, connect through Chicago, fly to Iowa, do my sound check, and perform the show. That did not happen. Instead, I flew to Miami where I found myself facing a delayed flight. I realized that if that flight was delayed that I would probably miss my flight to Iowa. At this point most people would have turned into a person known as "Negative Nancy." She is the negative person who always looks at the problems and never the solutions. I, however, chose to close my eyes and say those magical words, "I CHOOSE to be happy." At that moment no outside influence could change my mood. I was in control. The happiness came from within.

I immediately changed my flight to connect through Houston instead of Chicago. When I got there, my flight to Iowa was delayed. I again changed my flight. Then it all collapsed…a third flight was delayed. At that point there was no option. I was going to miss the show. The universe did not want me to perform. That day, I landed in Iowa a few hours after my show was supposed to start. It was snowing. It was cold. I was supposed to be relaxing on the beach sipping on an exotic drink. I checked into my hotel, laid in my bed, and pondered the fact that I just flew halfway around the world for absolutely nothing. This was only the third show in over 20 years that I missed. (A good record if I do say so) The fact still remained that it was a horrible chain of events.

The next day I flew out of Iowa having accomplished nothing other than escaping without frostbite from the winter chill. Despite all of that, I was happy. I focused on the simple moments. I chose happiness. The moral of this story is to remind you that outside influences do not determine your mentality. You do. You're not a baby anymore. Don't look to the outside world for happiness anymore. You are old enough to realize that you have a choice on how you react to the outside world. When you learn to choose happiness, you silence all the noise in the world. It is then that you can focus on your vision of the future.

Side note: In case you were wondering. I simply rescheduled a new date for the performance, flew back, and performed to a very enthusiastic crowd. Everything was good…and it continues to be good…because I say so.

23. I'm Naked Right Now

I'm typing this as I lay in a bed onboard a cruise ship somewhere off the coast of Antigua in the Caribbean. I removed all of my clothing, kicked back, and began typing. On the television in the background is a biography of the famous painter Paul Gauguin. As I lay here I'm thinking about a time when the famous and infamous Uri Geller gave me advice. You may know his name from his ability to bend spoons with his mind. During the 1970's Uri Geller became famous for doing the impossible. A few years ago I was given the pleasure of befriending Uri Geller during the production of a TV show that we filmed together. I was later invited to his home. We ended up going to dinner together and during the walk back to his penthouse I asked Uri a question that I will forever remember the answer given. I asked Uri to give me advice. I didn't give any restrictions to the question and therefore allowed him to interpret the reasons behind the question. His answer was two-fold but simple. He said "Invest in real estate and cause controversy" In the years since he told me these things I've realized the power in his words.

If you think back throughout your own life there are few people that have made an impact on you. Of course those family members who are genetically linked to you no doubt had an effect. However, beyond that, only those who have caused some sort of "controversy" or major emotional impact have had an influence on your life. I like to think of simple examples to prove my point. Imagine yourself in an elevator filled with strangers. There is often "the guy" in the elevator. He is the guy who breaks the unwritten rule of riding in an elevator. The unwritten rule is that you aren't supposed to talk to anyone in an elevator. I think that's why someone came up with the idea of elevator music. It's to break the uncomfortable silence that lingers in the air. Occasionally you find "the guy" who decides to strike up a random conversation. The interesting thing is that the guy who decides to speak is the guy you will remember. Everyone else fades away like an extra in a movie.

I think back to the last elevator rise I took and it was the guy who made silly comments that I remember. If you asked me who else was on the ride, I wouldn't be able to tell you. But that one guy stands out like a sore thumb. The question remains: "How does that apply to me?" The answer is simply: Be the guy who talks in the elevator and you will lead a more fulfilling life. If you fall into the same current as the silent lemmings of the earth, you will fade away like the sun setting. Nobody will remember. However, if you speak up and cause controversy you will be able to cause a ripple in the norm. It is a deep-seeded need for all humans to create a meaning to their lives. As of this moment, no man knows why we are here. However, we are genetically programmed to create our legacy on this planet. We all strive to procreate, leave behind heirs, and leave behind a legacy that will be remembered.

"Cause controversy" was one of the best pieces of advice I ever received. The people in my life that has caused controversy are the ones who have made an impact. To live in a world of comfort is to live in a world devoid of color. You can sit in your room and lay in your bed your entire life. You can be comfortable. You can be content. But lack of adventure and controversy creates a complacency that leaves a human being utterly useless.

An interesting idea that recently dawned on me is: "Live life like you're going to die one day." You can take that one to the bank.

As human beings we like to become stale. It's human nature to get comfortable in routines. You do it every day. Even tomorrow you'll do it again. You'll wake up and do the same routine you've been doing for years. Every time you step in the shower you more than likely wash yourself in the same order every single time. I personally start by shampooing my hair, rinse, add conditioner. I let the conditioner sit while I wash my chest, then left arm, right arm and so on. If you don't wash yourself in the same order every time you shower then perhaps you've been victim to "white line fever". This is where you were driving, perhaps a route you take often, and when you reach your destination you snap out of some sort of trance and can't remember driving at all. The entire route you drove is a lost set of actions that you could never recall.

If you ever wondered if you could be hypnotized and you've experienced that, the answer is yes. You can be hypnotized. In that moment in the shower or in the car when you "zoned out", you hypnotized yourself. You stepped into a world of complacency. Even after you read this you will continue to do so. The key to leading a successful and exciting life is step outside of those moments, realize they exist, and make an active effort to cause controversy. Do something different. Do something every day that will scare the shit out of you. If you do, you will look back and have memories of an exciting life.

Uri Geller told me that he measured the newspaper articles written about him in inches. In other words, it didn't matter what people were saying about him. It was the length of the article that mattered. Evaluate your own life and ask yourself "How many articles could be written about my life?" If the answer is not many, then it's time to make changes in your script. Lead the type of life that people can write stories about. Be the person that people will talk about when you leave the elevator. Otherwise you will just be along for the ride. I'd prefer to be the conductor. Be the author of your own story…the one who writes it in the nude.

24. Beauty Is In The Eye...

The year was 2000. I was a freshman at a small college in Pennsylvania studying business management. As part of the curriculum I had to take a psych 101 course. During the course my professor, who knew my background in magic, approached me and asked me to do a presentation on sensation and perception. The general concept that what we see and sense controls what we think. Of course I kindly obliged my professor, hoping for a better grade. During my presentation I explained to the class that magicians would often use a common object to fool their audience. These objects include, but are not limited to, a box, a length of rope, a deck of cards, etc. What the magician relies on to fool us is our perception and assumptions that we create when we see an object. To demonstrate this idea I brought out a shoebox with a lid on it. I showed it to the class and asked them what they thought I was holding. Everyone of course answered, "A shoebox." When I asked them to describe the shoebox in detail some of the descriptions were in fact perceptions rather than fact. One of the students commented that it had five sides and a lid. In that moment I turned the shoebox around to show that the backside of the shoebox was indeed missing. This would allow me to secretly insert or remove objects from the box while it still had the lid on.

You may be wondering what the purpose of this story may be. The fact of life is similar to the story of the shoebox. Perception creates reality. The way people perceive us will inevitably determine our success in both our personal and business lives. If your children perceive you as an idiot, you, by default, are an idiot. If your neighbor believes you are a multi-billionaire who secretly hoards his money...you are a multi-billionaire in that person's mind. The question remains as to whether or not people's perception can create reality. I believe it can.

As a professional magician I have spent most of my life creating routines to entertain people. This creative process usually begins with the end in mind. I have to figure out what impossible thing I want the audience to see. Whether it is to walk on water, levitate five feet in the air, or make an audience member vanish in mid air. Regardless of the method, I have to create the ending first and reverse engineer it. I first look at what magicians call the "effect." This is the effect that it has on the audience, aka what they perceive. After I come up with the ending I ask myself "How can I make the audience believe that is what they experienced?" I don't have to actually create the experience. I just have to make them believe that they witnessed it.

In the same way that I reverse engineer that experience for an audience, I believe we can reverse engineer our lives. Often times what the people around us perceive becomes our reality. I can remember a time, long ago, when I was in high school. There was a girl who was known as the class "slut." Everyone would always comment how that particular girl would lay down and have sex with anyone who wanted it. To this day I know that many of my classmates still believe that is the truth. However, I knew the girl personally and I knew that she was in fact extremely religious and remains a virgin to this day.

Everyone's perception created this girl's identity, just the way that I created that story. Everything I just presented to you was a story I made up. I'm sitting on a plane from Chicago to Los Angeles and made that entire story on the fly as I was typing. In the moment you first read the story I assume that you believed me. You made the assumption that I actually experienced the story that I fed you. You assumed.

Now take that same idea and apply it to your life. The way people perceive you will often drive their thoughts and actions to move you closer to their perception of you. I know many of you may say "I don't care what people think about me." Yes, yes. I know, I know. Calm down. In the grand scheme of things it may not matter what people think about you. However, it does matter during our day-to-day experiences when it comes to your interactions.

Take for instance a job interview. If you are a graduate student and are highly educated, you may qualify for a high-paying job. Now imagine you walk into the interview wearing stained sweatpants, a sleeveless T-shirt with the words "I hate people" printed across the front. Let's also imagine you arrived forty minutes late and your excuse was that your drug dealer didn't pick you up on time. I'm sure we can both agree that your interviewer will probably not rate you a good candidate for the job. The reality remains that you are more than qualified and the story you told, verbally and non-verbally, created a reality in that person's mind. Granted their reality may be false, but in this case that perception cost you a job.

Right now I just finished an ice cream covered brownie for dessert. I'm currently sitting in first class and am enjoying the amenities that come with it: free alcoholic beverages, dinner, warm assorted nuts, and flight attendants who cater to my every need. The perception of those people in coach may be that I paid a high price to sit here. I often hear people in airports comment how they would never pay the insane fees to sit in first class. I've heard people say that those in first class are just trying to "Show off." That type of person may look at me right now and say that I'm just wasting my money to show off. In fact, I didn't pay a dime to be here. I was upgraded completely free by the airline due to the fact that I'm a frequent flyer with the airline. This is yet another example of how people's perception can alter their judgment.

My friend Marc Elliot who is a fantastic speaker and author told me a story of his experience on a bus. The story as I can remember it is as follows. There was a man and his son sitting in the front of a bus. The little boy was screaming and throwing things around the bus. It was clear that everyone on the bus was annoyed with noise. It was even more frustrating to see the boy's father not reprimanding him for misbehaving. Everyone sat on the bus without saying a word and the boy continued to scream and yell. At one point a woman stood up, walked over to the boy's father and screamed, "Why don't you shut your kid up!" She said what everyone on the bus was thinking. At that moment the man looked at the woman and replied. "My son is crying and screaming because his mother just died. We are returning home from her funeral." The woman quietly sat down, ashamed of her outburst. Her perception of the experience on the bus forced her to take action. In the same way, what you deliver to the world will determine how the world responds. It could be positive, negative, active, or inactive.

What does this mean for you? The point of this section is to force you to open your eyes to the rest of the world and create a reality through the eyes of others. You must begin to become the person you are not only in your mind, but also through your interactions with others. If you desire to become a professional photographer then when asked what you do for a living, you should say, "I am a professional photographer." The person who asks you that question might then ask you for a business card in hopes of one day using your services. In their eyes and therefore reality, you are a professional photographer. If instead you say, "I'm a cashier at a grocery store" then you would not have handed out your contact information and in that moment, not become the person you desire to be.

As I described earlier, you must come FROM your goals and realize that you must infect people with your passion. Be the person you are. In the same way Michelangelo could see David in the block of stone and carved him free, you must see your future self in who you are and carve yourself free through the eyes of others. This mentality will be a catalyst to your success.

Let me point out that I believe in this theory as a practical path to success. As an addendum it's important to note that I'm not instructing you to lie. It's a fundamentally ignorant and morally abhorrent thing to lie. What I'm asking you to ponder is how you are being seem through the eyes of others. It is possible to maintain your income through a jog as a cashier while still carrying the title of "Professional Photographer." You are not truly limited by one aspect of your life. It is that belief that often holds people back from accomplishing great things.

I for one wear many hats. I am a professional mentalist. I'm also a professional illusionist. I am an author. I'm also a motivational speaker. If I'm engaging in a conversation with a person who books entertainment I will be more likely to mention that I am a mentalist & illusionist. If I'm talking to a person whose sole job is to hire speakers for their corporation, I will most likely mention that I'm a motivational speaker. This isn't dishonest. It's target marketing. I recommend that you use this same idea to your advantage. Remember to be aware of how people view you in your daily life. It will have tremendous and almost uncountable impact on your life. Remember, beauty is in the eye of the beholder.

25. You Might As Well Jump

Picture yourself driving down the road and you come to an intersection. When you approach the intersection the traffic light turns yellow. You have two options. I'm sure you're well aware of what those two options are. You can either gun it and fly through the yellow light at a break-neck pace, or you can choose to slow down and come to a stop. Both of those options are your choices. However, you often find those indecisive people who speed up and then change their mind and stop in the middle of the intersection. They shortly thereafter run the red light, narrowly avoiding being T-boned or they put their car in reverse and nearly smash into the car waiting behind them. I have a sneaking suspicion that you may have been in this position yourself at one point. There is a true lesson in these moments: Hesitation will get you killed. When I refer to hesitation I mean this in both the literal and figurative sense.

Often throughout life we come to a crossroad. We have to choose either A or B. Both may be viable options with outcomes that are both acceptable, but we hesitate. Too many times during these moments of hesitation, we lose an opportunity. For instance, I am currently on a plane heading from Dallas to Guatemala City. I boarded my flight about an hour ago. Prior to boarding the flight I was walking near my gate surfing the internet on my phone and I was sifting through one of my favorite social media sites. I instantly noticed a post from a celebrity's wife who was accompanying him on a trip to Spain. She mentioned she was at the airport in Dallas and wanted a copy of a new book that had just come out. She offered triple the book's value in cash to anyone who could bring her a copy at the airport's restaurant. She mentioned she was in terminal D. I was also in terminal D. I looked over and there they were. I couldn't believe my eyes.

There was an opportunity to walk over, introduce myself, and comment on the post she had just made. In my case, I could have then performed some magic or read their minds and certainly made a lasting impression. But I hesitated. I kept walking thinking about what I would say. Seriously over-analyzing. By the time I turned around and walked back, they were both gone. I hesitated and lost the opportunity.

If you have a moment of hesitation in a time sensitive opportunity, you will more than likely look back and say, "I should have…" Fill in the blank. Make sure you instantly grab a serendipitous gift when fate hands it to you. Don't hesitate. Please don't confuse me saying, "Don't hesitate" with "Don't think." Not thinking is just as bad as hesitating. Sometimes it can be worse. Take time to think and then pull the proverbial trigger.

The situation in the airport today might sound familiar to you. Perhaps you had an opportunity that slipped through your fingers and if you had to do it over again you would certainly choose differently. In fact, that was not my first scenario like that. I can remember a time when I was in Vegas with some good friends. We went to a nightclub and instantly spotted a major celebrity. I'm excluding names as to not date myself. I don't want you to be reading this book and say, "Man, this is old." Hopefully my mentions of surfing the internet on my phone didn't already date myself. I regress. While we were partying at the club and spotted the celebrity I noticed that he was very openly talking to fans and taking pictures with them. I again started thinking. Again, over-thinking. I began to think about what I was going to say, how I was going to say, whether or not I was going to shake his hand, what magic trick I would perform for him, the possible reactions he would have, what the people around him would think, and so on. By the time I finished calculating, he was gone. He left the club. Another opportunity to share my craft with someone I admired had disappeared faster than I could have made it vanish. I hesitated and I lost out.

Don't lose out. Take an average amount of time to ponder things that surprisingly fall into your lap and then act. Remember the last step in the four-part process? DO. I could feel, define, and plan all day. In the end the key step is in the action, the doing. This section hopefully reaffirms your understanding of the power of action. Dreams will remain dreams until you make an active effort to turn them into reality. Don't hesitate. Make it through the intersection in one piece. Satisfied and accomplished.

26. I Hate Accounting

"There are only two things in life that are guaranteed: death and taxes."

-

It's a famous saying that most of us have heard unless you've been living under a rock. You must file your taxes or hire an accountant to do it for you. Life on the other hand doesn't allow you to hire someone to do the accounting in your personal life. You must do your own accounting. In other words, you must be accountable for your actions.

By now you have hopefully set up an action plan for things that you want to accomplish. Perhaps you want to write your own book. Maybe you want to plan a trip that you've putting off. Regardless, you no doubt have something in your mind that you would like to do. The question remains: What happens if you don't do it? It's likely that the answer is "absolutely nothing." You will probably continue to live the same life you are currently living. The problem is that you won't be fulfilled. My recommendation is that you hold yourself accountable for the goals and visions that you set for yourself.

I've personally read many inspirational books that sent me into an emotional high. After reading them I was ready to take on the world. A month after reading the book I could feel myself slipping back into a state of comfortable staleness. I had set up visions of the future without setting up consequences if I didn't complete the goals I had set. No consequences. No results.

When I was a child my parents would often tell me to eat all of my food, clean my room, take out the trash, and other childhood norms. 99% of the time I did what I was told. The reason I did what I was told lies in the fact that my parents often had consequences. If I didn't do what I was told I would be grounded, not allowed to play with my friends, etc. I was held accountable. As we go through life most of the consequences are created by others, namely our parents or teachers. As we get older the accountability shifts from being created by outward sources to being created by ourselves.

As an adult, if I don't make my bed, my bed remains disheveled. If I don't take out my trash, my house will stink like a landfill. It is your responsibility to create consequences for yourself.

It might sound ridiculous to threaten to ground yourself for not completing your goals and I'm not suggesting that as an option. I am merely pointing out the fact that if you are not holding yourself accountable for your life commitments, then nobody else will. If you have unlimited self-motivation you may not need to worry about accountability. Perhaps you are the type of person who always does what they set out to do, congratulations. If you are in the other section of society who finds themselves involved in yo-yo dieting, unfinished projects on their desk, a to-do list older than it should be, or spring-cleaning that has yet to be completed, you need to hold yourself accountable. I'll leave it up to you to decide your own consequences. You are, after all, your own boss.

P.S. I know you shifted your food around your plate to make it look like you ate it. That doesn't work anymore. It's time to man up.

27. True Stories

Here are a few examples of people who have used this system with great success. Quite some time ago I got a phone call from a long time female friend of mine. She told me that she was sick of working her job as a waitress and wanted to pursue her passion of singing. I coached her through the system and the ideas that you've just read. But prior to doing so I asked her a few questions. I asked her what she wanted to do. She answered that she wanted to be famous. So I asked her what her definition of famous was. She said having her music on the radio, being on TV, and having stories written about her was her definition of famous. I continued by asking her exactly what radio station she wanted her music on. She replied with a radio station based in Miami, FL.

I then asked her what she felt was stopping her. She replied that she had no money. She went on about not being able to afford photo shoots and so on. I told her that she had every resource she could ever need in order to have everything she ever wanted. This girl, being a true-blood pessimist didn't believe me. Three weeks later, after following my system, she had her music played on the radio station she envisioned, had three newspaper interviews, had several photo shoots scheduled (at no cost), and was cast in a television show on MTV. Have faith in the ideas in this book. These ideas will change your life if you adopt them as a lifestyle.

Another girl who grew up in my hometown always told me her dream of becoming a playmate. The town we grew up in was just ranked as having the highest poverty rate in the country. Literally, ranked the poorest people in the United States of America. She gave up on her dream of modeling and fell into the monotonous lifestyle that everyone seems to turn to. Invited her to California so I could coach her and teach her the things you're now reading. She's been in California for just a few weeks and just had a test shoot with Playboy a few days ago. Listen to what I'm telling you. It works.

28. Ten Things to Remember

1. It's not what you know it's who you know, and more importantly, who knows you.

2. Marketing is just as important as talent.

3. Love what you do. Let it consume you and become part of your identity.

4. Always carry business cards with you.

5. Create deadlines for yourself. Work expands to fill the time up until it's deadline.

6. Those that are successful are the one's who don't stop trying. The rest didn't want it bad enough.

7. Talk to as many people who have already been where you are.

8. Read as many books as you can on what you want to accomplish.

9. Network as much as you can.

10. Remember to determine your core values. Base all decisions on those values.

29. Great Quotes To Ponder

"If you ask 1,000 people for something that you want, you'll get it."

-Byron Katie

"Commitment is continuing to move toward your goal, even when the feeling you have about it right now is gone."

-unknown

-If you want to have more, you have to become more. Success is not a *doing* process, it's a *being* process. Success is something that you attract by the person you become. For things to improve, YOU have to improve. For things to change, YOU have to change. When you change, everything changes for you.

-Jim Rohn

"Action is the foundational key to all success."

-Pablo Picasso

"Develop success from failures. Discouragement and failure are two of the surest stepping-stones to success. "

-Dale Carnegie

"I couldn't wait for success, so I went ahead without it."

-Jonathan Winters

"You have to work harder on yourself than you do on your job."

-Jim Rohn

Special Thanks

Rose Schober

Frederick Hoffman

Steve & Dorothy Colamarino

Anthony and Katherine Colamarino

Judy Colamarino

Tony Colamarino

Wayne Shifflett

Nick Gentry

Steve Hardison

Steve Chandler

Jim Rohn

Byron Katie

Stephen Covey

Scott Molluso

The University of Santa Monica

Ron and Mary Hulnick

Cabrini Academy

Holy Name High School

David Allen

Chris Hodgkins

Joshua Landis

Jeff Yalden

Wayne Dyer

Gary Mengel

Marc Elliot

Monique Weingart

Kourtney Reppert

Arielle Derouen

Will Rogers

Abraham Lincoln

Oprah Winfrey

Jerry "Earmuffs"

Lester Bahr

You

ABOUT THE AUTHOR

Wayne Hoffman is a professional mentalist and illusionist from Reading, Pa. He currently resides in Hollywood, Ca. He began his career as a performer and later found a passion for life coaching and motivational speaking. He travels the world presenting his entertainment shows and his motivational speech. He loves photography.

Made in the USA
Middletown, DE
06 September 2018